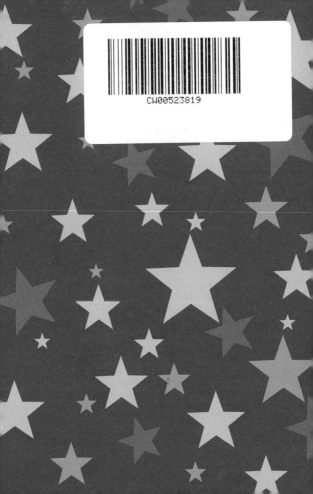

365 DAYS
★★★★★★★★ OF ★★★★★★★★
WISDOM

Yvette Jane

summersdale

365 DAYS OF WISDOM

Summersdale Publishers Ltd
46 West Street
Chichester
West Sussex
PO19 1RP
UK

www.summersdale.com

Printed and bound in the Czech Republic

ISBN: 978-1-84953-544-1

Substantial discounts on bulk quantities of Summersdale books are available to corporations, professional associations and other organisations. For details contact Nicky Douglas by telephone: +44 (0) 1243 756902, fax: +44 (0) 1243 786300 or email: nicky@summersdale.com.

To... **Dearest Fiona**

From... **Lesley**

Lots of Love
~ x ~

JANUARY

January is named after Janus who was worshipped as the Roman god of beginnings and transitions. He is depicted with two faces, one looking to the past, the other to the future. Make today the start of your quest to become wiser!

2 A resolution is the act of deciding on a course of action, something you are determined to embrace every day of your life. Perhaps this year's new resolution will be to live each day with wisdom.

Write a list of goals that you would like to achieve in your life and make a start on pursuing one of them today.

 Wisdom is gained from being open-minded to other people's ideas. Practise this art by mindfully listening in all your conversations today.

 Wisdom is not an off-the-shelf product you might buy in the January sales. Where you find it may sometimes surprise you; be observant and make this your year of wisdom and learning.

Seek not to follow in
the footsteps of the men
of old; rather, seek what
they sought.

Buddha

7

Wisdom is the under-rated necessity of life and the guardian of your success.

Bob Beverley

A wise person knows that gentleness is a powerful strength – practise simple acts today, such as offering advice with a kind heart to someone in need.

 Explore your own personal development by attending a new class or workshop in something that you've always longed to do. Be amazed at what you can learn about yourself.

 If you feel flustered today try to stay calm and remain true to yourself. Trust that this is a cornerstone towards your growth in wisdom.

Set aside some time to create a vision board to help you achieve your aspirations.

 Memorise some of the incisive quotes in this book and recite your favourites to yourself throughout the day.

 A sign of wisdom is wanting to share your knowledge with others – be a team player today and enjoy the results.

 Learn more about meditation, as it is a powerful means of developing your own inner wisdom.

15 If you're feeling overwhelmed, pause, take a deep calming breath and work out what really matters to you.

 16 Don't beat yourself up with 'should-haves', simply learn from your experiences and quietly affirm to yourself the phrase 'All is well'.

 17 Everybody's life journey is unique. Have courage to choose your own direction today – one that you feel is true to you.

18 A wise person acknowledges that there is always more to learn, experience and explore. Spend half an hour researching a topic that you have never investigated before.

 19 When spending time with family, consider the wisdom of children, as their viewpoints can be refreshing and honest.

 20 'Expertise' is not the same as wisdom. It is knowledge within a specific field, whereas wisdom is being at ease with what one knows and what one doesn't know.

21 Take time to ground yourself by focusing on your feet and connecting to the earth. Wisdom acknowledges we are all part of this one universe.

 22 Regularly spend a few minutes of contemplative thought in a peaceful place, allowing you the space to grow in wisdom and intuition.

 23 Stop, pause and reflect to consider a situation and its implications before you leap in straight away with hasty decisions.

Saying 'I don't know' to a question is not a sign of weakness, but of wisdom and honesty. Perhaps add, 'But I am open to finding out.'

 Acknowledge that wisdom is not about winning. Success means achieving the highest outcome for everyone.

 Keep it simple. Being rushed off your feet may appear to make you look the part, but it does not equate with wisdom.

Preconceived notions are the locks on the door to wisdom.

Merry Browne

True wisdom comes to each of us when we realise how little we understand about life, ourselves and the world around us.

Socrates

29 Yin and yang are complementary opposites, impossible to have one without the other. Remember to balance your day of work with some personal time.

 30 Notice how your mind fills with judgements today and recall how no one is above you or below you; with wisdom we have the awareness that we are all equal.

 31 If you want to introduce a new positive habit, make it a daily experience. It must become something you no longer question, something that grows into the structure of your life.

FEBRUARY

1 Listen mindfully to others; there is always something they can teach you, whether it's in the workplace, with family or with a loved one.

2 Dreams are said to reveal the deepest recesses of our lives. Interpret them with a book and be inspired by their meaning.

Hindsight and regret undermine the truth that you made your decisions with the knowledge and ability you had at that time. Be at peace with your choices.

 There is barely time for perception and discernment in a rushed and noisy environment. As you move around, walk slowly with a relaxed gait and a cheerful smile.

 Look for opportunities to be considerate today – if you're driving, allow others to enter the traffic queue or, when at work, ask a colleague who looks stressed if they need your help.

6 Listening to your inner voice will help you make wise decisions – sit in a quiet and undisturbed space in order to hear that wisdom come through.

 7 Be honest with yourself and acknowledge today what biases and prejudices you carry deep within you. It's a challenge to uproot them but begin by taking notice.

 8 Don't be afraid to ask questions – it really is a good way of learning. Try it out in public with strangers – you will be amazed at what you find out!

If we put into practice the things we have learnt from life our achievements might be an inspiration to others. Who will you inspire today?

 Make time to consider your physical well-being and give yourself a regular health audit. If you notice any part of you has not been feeling well for some time, investigate further, don't ignore it.

 Set aside time in your day to detach from the constant flurry of media like emails, Facebook, Twitter and television. Wisdom arises in quiet moments.

Become a member of Amnesty International, or something similar, and learn about those less fortunate than yourself.

 Conquer your fears so that fear doesn't conquer you – speak to someone to help you address something that may be holding you back.

Valentine's Day: Plan a day out with your favourite person and enjoy the magical moments we can often take for granted that arise simply from having fun together.

Release opinions, free yourself from views. Be open to mystery.

Jack Kornfield

The teacher who is indeed
wise does not bid you
to enter the house of his
wisdom but rather leads
you to the threshold of
your mind.

Kahlil Gibran

17 Ask questions of people you regard highly so that they may lend a helping hand to you in your work or family life.

 18 Appreciate the simplest of things as these are our daily miracles and allow us to develop wisdom in our hearts. Just open the curtains on arising and start from there.

 19 Make a list of your strengths and positive attributes; remind yourself that you are confident yet humble and this in turn will be noticed and respected by others.

Give yourself the time to reflect on your choices and experiences. This is how you develop your potential for self-growth.

 Problems and challenges in our lives are exactly the places where we can gain wisdom from our experiences. Embrace them!

 Being patient is always a wise move.

 Don't miss the chance to look up at the moon or the stars. A quiet moment spent noticing these wonders can quickly put life's chaos back into perspective.

Early to bed and early to rise, makes a man healthy, wealthy and wise.

Benjamin Franklin

25

Wise men talk because
they have something to
say; fools, because they
have to say something.

Plato

Set aside time to decide what is really important to you in your life. Sometimes brainstorming with friends can be a valuable way to discover new pathways.

 There are many books of wisdom from all over the world. Find an enlightening book to keep by your bedside and regularly dip into it.

28 Be open to the mystery and miracles we experience every single day – notice how often you could whisper to yourself 'wow'.

29

Leap Day: Leap into action and make plans to travel anywhere in the world, near or far – simply bring an inquiring mind and an open heart.

MARCH

1 Make time today to focus on your emotional well-being. Do not let emotions simmer; ignored they can boil over. Address the issues that you realise need to be resolved.

2 Visit an art exhibition to gain a different understanding and enjoyment of another's creative ideas.

The opposite of wisdom is folly – just ask yourself today as you are about to embark on something – am I being wise or could this be foolish?

 Be selective about what media you explore. Enhance your understanding of the world and always ask questions but don't get distracted by the temptations of social media.

 Be original – be flexible to listening to others, yet know your own mind.

Angry people are not always wise.

Jane Austen

There's no to-do list for creating a wisdom culture; there's only a to-be list.

Marianne Williamson

Don't be scared to take risks – if they work that's great, if they don't then you have become a little wiser.

 If you have tedious chores that need to be completed today, set your mind to think positively about the end results rather than the doing.

Mum

Bring a 'beginner's mind' to your day and see things afresh. Perhaps take a different route home and see things with a new perspective.

11 If you are faced with a problem, don't panic. If you calmly examine the issue, wisdom will prevail.

 12 Remember that staying silent can be a wise starting point while you allow space for your inner wisdom to emerge.

 13 Today's wise reminder is not to blame someone else when things go wrong. Own your decisions and show courage in acknowledging your share of the outcome.

 14 Myths, legends and folklore often contain nuggets of wisdom so sit back and enjoy a good story – book, film or audio.

Honesty is the first chapter in the book of wisdom.

Thomas Jefferson

The fool doth think he is wise, but the wise man knows himself to be a fool.

William Shakespeare

Socrates and other ancient philosophers believed in a philosophical life that encompassed a love of wisdom with a holistic way of living. Take a few moments to reflect on your personal lifestyle.

 To be wise is not necessarily to be enigmatic and complex but to be straightforward and clear in expression. Today check that you are saying what you really mean.

 Don't be scared to mull over ideas and ponder upon the outcome. A slow, considered approach is appropriate in many situations.

MARCH

20

To acknowledge the spring equinox, have a spring clean. Clear out the old and bring a fresh outlook into your life, acknowledging that collecting material things is not as rewarding as aspiring to wisdom.

21 Your mantra today is: 'I am prepared to face problems while remaining positive.'

22 Today notice how you may be tempted to complain. See if you can use these moments to learn more about yourself and your complaint may become unnecessary.

23 Sometimes our own thoughts can be obstacles to success. Make up your own phrases to recite to yourself when you lose your courage. 'I am strong and capable.' 'I am safe and protected.'

 24 A kernel of wisdom may appear amongst a wealth of worthless matter. Look out for one today!

 25 Be aware that we all hold preconceived ideas. Avoid listening to rumours you may hear today and wait for the truth to surface.

Challenge yourself to the use of new vocabulary – perhaps learn and use one new and exciting word a week?

 When you feel too irritated by something or someone, do nothing until you have reached a position of calm.

 Set yourself wise goals for life and encourage and reward your progress.

 Learn to love both your strengths and weaknesses – be accepting and compassionate of both yourself and other people. Take special notice of this today.

30 The three wise monkeys are said to depict wisdom with their expressions 'See no evil', 'Speak no evil' and 'Hear no evil'. Perhaps start today with a plan of 'no gossiping'.

 31 See everyday pleasures through eyes of gratitude – everything from your comfortable bed, hot water and clean clothes, to the early morning mist and the dawn chorus.

APRIL

April Fool's Day: Happy, joyful people are an inspiration – the Dalai Lama combines his great wisdom with constant good humour. Don't forget to giggle at least once today!

 Plants contain the wisdom of nature. If you have access to a garden, an allotment or a windowbox, plan a grow-your-own project. Grow camomile or mint to make herbal teas and strawberries for eating at breakfast.

Knowing yourself is the beginning of all wisdom.

Aristotle

The saddest aspect of life right now is that science gathers knowledge faster than society gathers wisdom.

Isaac Asimov

APRIL

 If you are feeling unsure about a decision find a place of inner and outer calm before you make your choice. This could mean a quiet stroll in the fresh spring air.

 Today have a look to see if you can turn a small failure into a big success. This could be through a willingness to negotiate, and an acknowledgement that you made mistakes.

 Maybe you're feeling anxious about something. Don't resist what is happening to you, rather accept and welcome change in all its forms.

Forgiveness is a wise way forward. Sit quietly, focus on your breathing and on your heart. Trust that the harshness you may be feeling will eventually dissolve.

 Take advantage of the milder spring weather and plan a walk somewhere new. The unknown is full of learning opportunities, even if it's just to discover a new building, a hidden stream or a misshapen tree.

 A wise person cares about people, animals and the environment. See where you could make choices that reflect this and join causes that promote long-term views as opposed to short-term gains.

Turn your wounds into wisdom.

Oprah Winfrey

The simple things are also
the most extraordinary
things, and only the wise
can see them.

Paulo Coelho

Create some space in your mornings, either to relax with a cup of tea or sit in quiet contemplation. This gives you a regular time for the wisdom of your soul to speak to you.

 Notice the wondrous changes emerging around you as winter transforms into spring.

 Today make a point of listening with care, so that you truly hear what another person is saying to you.

Today give without the need for thanks or reciprocation. You could buy a coffee for a homeless person, help a stranger with directions or pass on your unused parking ticket to someone else.

 To seek wisdom is to look within and to trust your own awareness. Start a journal in which you record your daily experiences, decisions and thoughts.

 Close your eyes for a moment and notice what you hear. Just this simple act can allow a little extra space for wisdom.

APRIL

 19 If you have decided to make changes in your life, find blogs and books that inspire you and supportive online communities. It's tougher to change habits surrounded by people who don't want to change.

 20 Being extremely busy may mean that you haven't made the best choices to prioritise what is most important. Be clear today about your priorities and give yourself space to do them with your full attention.

 21 If you plan to go for a walk or run today, don't take music. Allow the quiet to give you space and opportunities for your thoughts and wisdom to surface.

22 Make time for the people who are closest to you. Sometimes our children and partners experience our grumpy, tired selves so be attentive and loving.

 23 Plan a reorganisation of your work surroundings. Create a tranquil space so you can fully focus on your tasks, be more productive and waste less time.

 24 Try a yoga, t'ai chi or chi kung class. These gentle ways of movement combine the wisdom of their history with the mindfulness they encourage you to bring to your physical body.

25 You don't always need to have the last word. If there is someone who presses your buttons, either at work or within your family, be curious as to why you feel strong reactions to them.

 26

Earth Day: Plant a tree. This is a contribution to the environment and symbolises your positive acceptance and trust that it may continue to grow to magnificence even after you have gone.

 27 See your life with wise eyes – be open to new ideas and collaboration.

28 Life is tough but we all have the chance to shine. Listen to a piece of music or read a poem to remind yourself that you can be wise and inspiring.

 29 Take special notice of your actions today and give yourself time to explore the reasons and meanings of your choices. This is how personal transformation occurs.

 30 'Philosophy' is composed of the Greek word philo meaning 'the love of' and sophia meaning 'wisdom'. Continue your journey of wisdom relishing every aspect of learning.

Simple and mundane tasks, such as doing the washing-up and tidying your home can seem humdrum. Complete them with focus and attention and they become opportunities for peace and acceptance.

 On waking today, notice your thoughts. Be aware of following the same habits that lead to dissatisfaction. This is the first step to making positive changes in your life.

Plan to walk a big hill or mountain. At the top you'll see things from a different angle. Allow yourself time up there to explore issues in your life that could benefit from a fresh approach.

 The women of Bengal use the folk art of stitching pictorial stories onto their quilts, depicting their feelings, dreams and wisdom for future generations. Can you create something that expresses yourself?

 Wisdom is like perfection – you may aspire to it but never reach it. Be OK with that.

Plan a day with friends learning a new activity like rock climbing, surfing or canoeing. It can be a way to build your courage and strength, offering a great challenge that's out of your comfort zone.

 Relax your shoulders and empty the thoughts running round in your mind. Wisdom comes when you're at peace.

 Stretch your mind, it's more elastic than you think. This could be simply by saying yes to something you would ordinarily say no to.

9 Be mindful today – choose to return to the present moment when you notice your thoughts have become nostalgic about the past or anxious for the future.

 10 Runes are an ancient alphabet consisting of symbols used by the Vikings to divine wisdom and meaning in all of their everyday experiences. Trust your own intuition as it is your personal path to wisdom.

 11 If today is turning out to be challenging, remember that life will always have its ups and downs. Try writing a list of potential ways to turn the negatives into positives.

Any fool can criticise, condemn and complain, and most fools do.

Benjamin Franklin

Knowing others is intelligence; knowing yourself is true wisdom.

Lao Tzu

Throughout the day ask yourself, 'Am I acting wisely now?'

 Turtles and tortoises are regarded as symbols of wisdom and patience in folklore all over the world. Find a keepsake to remind you of this.

 Be yourself – the real you is irresistibly unique. Rejoice in your favourite music, individual style, the hobbies you love and your personal world.

 Unlearning old habits can be painful but it's necessary to challenge assumptions and stale ways of thinking. What might you do differently today?

Go outside – take notice of nature's wisdom. All happens in good time; the sun doesn't set before it needs to and the flowers bloom at precisely the right moment.

 Learn lessons from history – yours and that of humankind. If you are able to, find out more about your own family tree and the lives your ancestors lived.

 Make space in your day to think about the plans you need to make if you want something in your life to change, otherwise they won't.

The older I grow,
the more I distrust the
familiar doctrine that
age brings wisdom.

H. L. Mencken

The desire to reach
for the stars is ambitious.
The desire to reach
hearts is wise.

Maya Angelou

23 If you are working with others today and have difficult issues to resolve, examine these challenges from all sides. Listen carefully to everyone's views.

 24 Focus your mind today to find some beauty in everything around you. You could be in the noisiest, busiest, most polluted city in the world but it can be found.

 25 Remember this little trick – focus on the positive and it will spread to others.

26 Don't forget you are a human being not a human doing. Scatter moments of tranquillity throughout your day to reclaim your balance, from extra slow breaths to a walk round the block.

 27 An act of kindness can provide the most memorable moment in a person's day. Be alert to opportunities to practise the true value of this.

 28 You have been given a life, what do you choose to do with it? Mull this question over today and look out for signs that may indicate a new direction you could take.

Be willing to take on risks even when the outcome may be uncertain. Approach today with bravery and alertness.

 Do not assume a single thing. Today ask yourself if there is something in your life that you need to re-evaluate.

 It is said that Buddha found enlightenment and wisdom as he sat beneath the Bodhi Tree. Find a tree you enjoy sitting beneath and make it your place to experience calm.

JUNE

 Be aware when you find you are putting up defences through comfort eating, drinking extra alcohol or working late again. Keep a diary to decipher how your emotions are linked to your habits.

 Being wise is no use to you unless you put it into practice, and better still, share it. Friends and family get to benefit, and in turn, you can learn from them.

JUNE

 Start your day listening to a different radio station from usual and continue making alternative choices as your day opens up. Shake yourself free from your usual habits!

 Wisdom is a state of mind. To develop wisdom you must be clear about your own set of values. These will infuse all that you say and do.

 Go somewhere nearby you have never visited before. Let this mini adventure awaken you to new experiences and fresh scenery.

Keep going at your own pace, steady and grounded, like the wise tortoise.

 Hindsight can allow all of us to be wise! List every good thing happening in your life right now, allowing today's abundance to triumph over all your past mistakes.

 A wise person brings out the best in another, and overlooks their faults. Make a big effort to try this today.

Make each day both useful and pleasant, and prove that you understand the worth of time by employing it well.

Louisa May Alcott

Never mistake knowledge
for wisdom. One helps you
make a living, the other
helps you make a life.

Sandra Carey

JUNE

 As you begin a new project take your time; haste may only bring short-term advantages. Be discerning enough to know that a measured approach will bring a better accomplishment in the long term.

 The phrase 'putting yourself in another's shoes' is a reminder for us all – everybody's views have blind spots so listen and learn.

 If today is already looking fraught try not to make any important decisions. Box them away and revisit them when you have a clearer, more logical outlook.

JUNE

 Awake each morning and know that every day is full of potential. Go for it!

 Look to future consequences of your actions as they can have far-reaching results. Get as much advice as you can if you are in the process of making important decisions in your life.

 Wisdom ranks as one of the six ingredients required for happiness alongside sincerity, integrity, humility, courtesy and charity. Write these words out and stick them on your computer or fridge door as daily reminders.

17 We are constantly learning but we must continually unlearn too. Notice which of your bad habits feel almost impossible to stop! This is the first step to making positive changes.

 18 Be an observer today – of others and of yourself. Recognising other people's reactions and emotions can provide helpful insights about how to approach difficult situations.

 19 Collective wisdom is a historical pool of experience, patterns and knowledge to which we all belong. Watch a film from another part of the world to gain a new perspective.

JUNE

 20 Value opportunities you may have to get feedback and opinions from work colleagues, friends and family. A deeper perspective is more likely to yield a wiser, all-round outcome.

 21

World Music Day: Choose a piece of classical music; something totally new to you or a favourite. Listen to it without any distractions and allow the sound to open your mind and heart. Carry this with you into your day.

 22 Read about other cultures and worldwide organisations to expand your understanding and dispel any limited thinking you may have. You could set yourself this as a long-term challenge!

JUNE

 23 Replace one of your usual coffees or teas with a herbal or green tea today. Be very aware of how challenging this might be and open up to these small changes.

 24 Become a world expert on you! You can help this process along by writing down thoughts and ideas regularly in a notebook or journal.

 25 Ayurveda is the wisdom of traditional Hindu medicine meaning 'knowledge of life'. It combines the well-being of body, mind and spirit balanced alongside nature. Find a local specialist to help you with replenishing Ayurvedic treatments.

Few problems are solved alone. If you cannot share with a friend, seek counselling to help shift any burden that might be weighing you down. Wisdom is not afraid to ask for support.

 Our deepest needs are universal and since peace is undeniably one of them, recite to yourself as often as you can remember today, 'I breathe in peace, I breathe out peace.'

 Sometimes it helps to just stop and listen to birdsong from outside. It allows you to reconnect with nature and to what is real and true.

29

Knowledge is proud that he has learn'd so much; Wisdom is humble that he knows no more.

William Cowper

Knowledge comes but wisdom lingers.

Alfred, Lord Tennyson

JULY

1 Certainty is an illusion as life often unfolds in unexpected ways. Do something unexpected for others today.

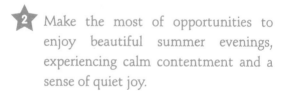

2 Make the most of opportunities to enjoy beautiful summer evenings, experiencing calm contentment and a sense of quiet joy.

When facing challenges, discern the difference between what you can change and what can't be changed. Address the things that are in your control.

 Allow yourself time to enjoy the warmer summer days by sitting outside on your break time or having a lunchtime picnic.

 Find out more about solar panelling or other energy-saving ideas and inform yourself about lifestyle alternatives. The choices we all make today are what create the future world.

The foolish man seeks happiness in the distance, the wise grows it under his feet.

J. Robert Oppenheimer

A loving heart is the truest wisdom.

Charles Dickens

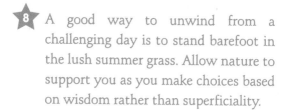

8 A good way to unwind from a challenging day is to stand barefoot in the lush summer grass. Allow nature to support you as you make choices based on wisdom rather than superficiality.

9 Reading a good biography can give you insights into another person's experiences. You can draw parallels with your own life, or learn from their life events.

10 Be passionate about something that you do. Your enjoyment and sharing of that can be an inspiration to others. Ask yourself what you like doing best in life.

You know you have gained wisdom when you recognise the old negative version of you in other people's behaviour. Give yourself a moment today for reflection about how you are evolving.

 A reminder today to take a wise approach to challenges: stay calm with slow, centred breaths. Open an extra window to breathe in the fresh summer air.

 Good old-fashioned words of wisdom: Always be polite!

An optimist is a person who sees a green light everywhere. The pessimist sees only the red light. But the truly wise person is colour-blind.

Albert Schweitzer

15

A wise man is superior
to any insults which can
be put upon him, and the
best reply to unseemly
behaviour is patience
and moderation.

Molière

16 The great Native American chiefs foretold the fundamental need for conservation to ensure the balance of life on earth. Join one of the many conservation or wildlife groups in support of our earth.

 17 Find sources of wisdom that you can turn to in times of need – this could be a trusted friend or a book whose author you respect.

 18 Humans strongly dislike being wrong. A wise reaction embraces the capacity to admit you could be wrong.

JULY

 19 Plan a trip to the swimming baths, lido or sea and surrender your tensions to the water, floating and yielding to the water's support. Bring this willingness to surrender with you into your day.

 20 Embrace opportunities from the smallest action to the biggest of challenges – take on life in all its forms as you head into today.

 21 Writing regularly in a journal is a great way to reflect on your experiences and choices, offering perspective and increasing your wisdom.

22 Be willing to focus on unravelling pertinent threads of detail today, but without forgetting the bigger picture.

 23 Give yourself the opportunity to correct your mistakes, even if it's just to re-paint the bedroom from bright magenta to calming blue.

 24 The wisdom of the Australian Aboriginal peoples includes the term dadirri, meaning 'deep listening'. It is the connection we make deep within our hearts and results in a quiet, still awareness.

 25 Make plans for what you wish to accomplish in life with a 'bucket list'.

Some of the wise things we learn with age are incommunicable to someone in their youth. Be patient the next time you are in this situation and try to help them understand.

 Any kind of fighting or war is a sign that humans have not referred to wisdom. Bear that in mind next time you feel the urge to shout in anger; take a pause and refrain!

 Start a gratitude diary where you jot down every blessing in your life. If you're really observant it won't take long to fill the pages of your diary.

29 Are you surrounded by advancing science and technology in the form of Internet connections, smartphones, tablets and e-readers? Slow down and find time to write a letter to a friend or relative.

 30 Plan a picnic or barbeque so that you can enjoy being outside in nature along with family and friends. It's a wise decision to give yourself time to appreciate the important things in life.

 31 Go for a walk where you can escape from the humdrum of everyday life and let your mind breathe.

AUGUST

 The lion represents power, wisdom and justice. If you love wild cats like the lion, place a photo or painting of one nearby to remind you of your inner wisdom and strength.

 Look out for the marvellous and the beautiful in unexpected places. Embrace all your senses as you sit and people-watch from a cafe or on a park bench.

AUGUST

 At the end of the day review how it went. Decisions, obstacles and unexpected events are all in the mix for you to see how discerning you have been!

Friendship Day: Get some friends together and join a local pub quiz – sharing knowledge is fun and enjoyable. Wisdom reveals itself by choosing not to drink too many pints.

 Conventional wisdom can sometimes box you in. Even if your work is a little uninspiring, find ways at home to be innovative, creative and larger than life.

Wisdom works in tandem with your heart. Trust what you carry within, knowing that you have a treasure to tap into by being still and quiet.

 A wise person is open to seeing good in everyone. Take this perspective today, being generous and good-humoured with all you meet.

 Take a second out in your day to remember to value yourself and what you do, with a deep, clearing breath and a glance up at the summer sky. There is wisdom in knowing your worth.

Be happy. It's one way of being wise.

Colette

A wise man makes his own decisions, an ignorant man follows public opinion.

Chinese proverb

AUGUST

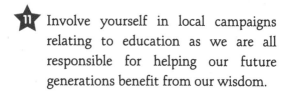

11 Involve yourself in local campaigns relating to education as we are all responsible for helping our future generations benefit from our wisdom.

12 If you are waiting to hear for results or an outcome, sit still, know that nothing more can be done and release your worries like a dandelion seed on the breeze.

13 Check through your possessions and pick out a couple of items you could give to a charity. It's a great way to lighten yourself of clutter and material stuff.

AUGUST

 14 A wise person takes responsibility for their own beliefs. Why not start discussions with a group of friends and get everyone to share their thoughts on big subjects like politics and religion?

 15 Spend an afternoon in the library reading up on Ancient Greek mythology as it is steeped in wisdom and amazing tales.

 16 Give yourself time to daydream, a flash of insight or a moment of intuition may well follow. If it worked for Einstein and Newton, it can work for you!

Our lives begin to end the day we become silent about things that matter.

Martin Luther King Jr

The highest form of wisdom is kindness.

The Talmud

Wisdom is nothing without integrity – are you being honest with yourself and others? Maybe it's time to sit down with somebody and have that heart-to-heart chat.

 Verbal repetition can help clarify an idea. The Roman amora (spokesman) Simeon ben Lakish would repeat any new insight 40 times to absorb the concept fully.

 Visit a church, temple or monastery in order to spend a few hours relaxing in the subdued and holy atmosphere. Come away with a calm sense of wisdom and tranquillity.

Although often depicted with Minerva, the goddess of wisdom, the owl is not actually a wise animal. Its brain is small yet it can focus quickly from near to far objects, making it an excellent hunter. Know your own strengths and build on those.

 Ensure your holidays include time for you to relax and recharge your batteries. Plan time for walks in the countryside and by the sea, afternoon teas, a spa visit and time spent with family.

 Look up at the changing clouds as a reminder that nothing stays the same.

Bake a cake to share at work. It's a lovely way to connect with your colleagues and everyone gets to enjoy your baking skills!

 Intuition is called our sixth sense. It's an immediate source of information enabling us to assess the truth of a situation in an instant. Don't forget your sixth sense today.

 Did you know you could increase your mental agility through eating plenty of vitamin C-rich foods such as blackcurrants, citrus fruit and green vegetables?

AUGUST

 28 Remember you can choose to switch off the radio and television, allowing the relative silence to offer some peace to your soul.

 29 Find a creative and light-hearted approach to getting people on board with your ideas. Force tends to be less successful.

 30 Today imagine you are carrying a magnifying glass. Examine everything with caution and notice every detail.

 31 Most situations can be observed from a number of perspectives – there's never one right way, just a way.

SEPTEMBER

 Self-growth is your greatest investment. Find out about some evening classes and events in your area and gain twice as much value through learning something new and making new friends.

 Query your judgements today. Taking a second glance over decisions may help you pick up on careless mistakes.

 Do no harm.

Don't waste time trying to alter things that cannot be changed. Enjoy your vibrant life to the full.

 Have you ever been horse riding? Book a lesson to experience travelling like the wise winged horse Pegasus of Ancient Greece.

 Make the decision that you will learn something new from everyone you meet today.

Never go to a doctor whose office plants have died.

Erma Bombeck

One's first step in wisdom
is to question everything –
and one's last is to come
to terms with everything.

Georg Christoph Lichtenberg

Having a dialogue with another person is a form of conversation where each is on a level footing without creating a power dynamic. Be mindful to see if that's what you are doing today.

 Boost your mental performance with a daily fish oil supplement, such as Omega 3.

 Dolphins are a symbol of wisdom and guidance. If swimming with dolphins has always been your dream, start planning to make this come true.

 Ask yourself this today, 'Am I being caring and compassionate?'

SEPTEMBER

 Foster your wisdom by reading on sundry themes and subjects. You could even explore the possibility of joining a reading club to share and discuss everyone's viewpoints.

 A kōan is an ancient puzzle or parable presented by the Zen teacher to his students to develop their wisdom and Zen practice. Have some fun exploring such kōans and the wisdom they contain.

 Arrange a posy of flowers in a jug and place it where you can gaze on it frequently. It can also provide a regular reminder of beauty, nature and optimism.

Knowledge is a process of piling up facts; wisdom lies in their simplification.

Martin Fischer

Wisdom is bright, and
does not grow dim.
By those who love her she
is readily seen,
and found by those who
look for her.

The Book of Wisdom, 12–13,
The Old Testament

Life is contained in the present moment. Each moment makes up our lives. Be aware today that all your moments are how you would like them to be.

 A calm morning ritual allows you to start your day from a place of advantage and sagacity. Try introducing a few minutes of meditating, yoga exercises or t'ai chi moves and notice the benefits.

 As you embark upon your day, approach tasks with a whole heart and with joy, being content that you know what you can achieve.

SEPTEMBER

 In West Africa, the symbol for wisdom is the spider's web, representing the creativity and complexities required to live a wise life. How are you spinning your web of life today?

International Day of Peace: Spend the day being peaceful. Move gently with grace and encourage your heart to send peaceful blessings to everyone around the globe.

 Choose seasonal fruits to eat and share with your family. It provides a great reminder of our connection to the earth and the miracle of fresh produce.

24 Look out for the wisdom of wonder when you notice such marvellous things as dewdrops, rainbows and frogs crossing your path.

 25 How can you put all your learning to good use today? Notice if there are instances when you can be of service to others and explore the option of volunteering.

 26 The very wisest of choices is to look after your health. Today make sure you are taking care of this with diet, exercise and rest.

SEPTEMBER

 27 You reveal your wisdom to others, not by following them, but by being your own person.

 28 When faced with a challenge, think back to a previous experience, remembering what you did then, and extract the wisdom from that.

 29 Notice the tendency you might have for striving and controlling when perhaps today you could experience going with the flow with ease and calm.

 30 Be compassionate and kind towards yourself and that will naturally spill out to everyone else you meet.

OCTOBER

 Observe the changing colours on the trees, knowing that nature reflects the seasons in your life.

 Be kind to yourself. Book time off to do what you love, so that you can return to your work energised and refreshed with a new perspective on things.

Technology provides a myriad of convenient ways to learn new skills and knowledge, by using a specialised app or software, or enrolling on a distance learning course. Spend an evening exploring your options.

World Smile Day: Smile at strangers today and see the wisdom and light in the eyes of other people. Notice what results this brings.

 Stay open to new ideas. One germ of a thought can lead you towards bigger things.

Be inspired by the German philosopher of the 1700s, Immanuel Kant. He encouraged people to 'dare to know' – to be autonomous in their thinking rather than relying on the knowledge of others.

 Don't say, 'I'm no good at that.' If you lack confidence in art, for example, buy some paints or pencils and play around with colour and techniques. Enjoy your new pastime!

 If you have been thinking about doing something for a long time, make today the moment to follow it through with action. What have you got to lose?

Choose a day to get things clutter-free. Whether at home or at work, this helps maintain clarity, without which wisdom can be obscured.

 Sometimes, simple and meaningful truths come from unexpected sources. Do not judge a person or a place by appearances.

 There are no magic solutions. Work hard and when you make mistakes be sure to learn from them.

Don't look where you fall, but where you slipped.

African proverb

The wise man shows no fear in the face of the unexpected, and no anger in the face of wrongful accusations.

Chinese proverb

History holds an enormous resource of wisdom. Choose a historical figure and learn about how their contribution helped society's evolution.

 Ensure you enlist upon plenty of support when you have challenging tasks to fulfil.

World Food Day: Why not try a memory-boosting menu today; cook up a meal including eggs, soybeans or vegetables such as broccoli, cabbage and cauliflower?

Today's wise reminder is to know yourself well enough to be familiar with your strengths and your weaknesses so you don't take on something beyond your capabilities.

 Make a list of the people in your life that you respect most for their good judgement, experience and wisdom. Always know that you can approach them for their wise advice.

 Excessive worry is like a rocking chair, keeping you busy but getting you nowhere. Stand up now and take a step forward!

When we see men of worth, we should think of equalling them; when we see men of a contrary character, we should turn inwards and examine ourselves.

Confucius

21

He is a wise man who
does not grieve for the
things which he has not,
but rejoices for those
which he has.

Epictetus

OCTOBER

 You may be stuck in a job you hate, but fill the rest of your life with things that you love, making sure you find balance and contentment.

 Akrasia is the Greek term for when you know the right course of action and yet do not choose to do it. Don't worry; you're not the only one guilty of this!

 Whatever today brings, be flexible, like the bamboo grasses that bend in the wind.

 Keep it simple.

26 Bring a heightened sense of appreciation into your day. Others will enjoy receiving positive feedback and you are more likely to have a lot more fun.

 27 Be money-wise by comparing costs for all your essential utilities. The time spent re-arranging bills on the phone is worth it to make some valuable savings.

 28 Take a pause if you are confronted with someone who irritates or angers you. This moment of silence allows your deeper wisdom to provide you with a wise response.

Determine today that you will be fully present when you listen to colleagues and friends. Let's share our wisdom!

 Look out of the window and rest your eyes on the changing colours of the autumn leaves. Allow nature's patience and continual flow to inspire the same in you.

If you're carving a pumpkin today don't throw away the pumpkin seeds, since a daily handful can provide a good source of zinc, enhancing memory skills and thinking processes. Who would have thought!

NOVEMBER

1 A flowing stream is symbolic of wisdom. If you pass one by, stop for a moment to listen and absorb its expansive, clear and ever-changing vibrations.

2 Our parents and grandparents embody their own form of wisdom, but we tend to journey away from them before acknowledging they may have something to teach us. Keep in loving touch with your relatives.

NOVEMBER

 Take pleasure in your accomplishments. By bringing a wise humility to your life you are adding value to what you do.

Stress Awareness Day: Make sure you have some healthy ways of de-stressing such as meditation, exercise, drinking tea or taking a walk.

 Enjoy the autumn aromas of bonfires, damp leaves and rain-drenched earth. Value these precious experiences.

Always say thank you when you have been helped – buy the person a coffee, send them a little note or pay it forward by doing something helpful for someone else.

 Today encourage yourself to ask others for their viewpoint. This could help shift a firmly held idea – and open it up to a more expansive outcome.

 If your mind is becoming full of concerns and you can't stop ruminating, remember Buddhist wisdom to sit and meditate, clearing your mind to be like a vast and open sky.

As for me, all I know is that I know nothing.

Socrates

Do not say a little in many words but a great deal in a few.

Pythagoras

Be aware of your intentions since they create your future. Write down a positive phrase to remember such as, 'I am successful and I am at peace.'

 Sometimes it feels like we have to start our lives all over again – be courageous and go for it.

 Gandhi spent one day a week meditating even during the busiest political times of the British Empire in India. Give yourself regular meditation time to focus on the wisdom of your heart.

14 Have a brainstorming session with friends — create a list of 20 ways to make positive changes in your lives.

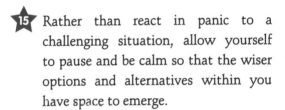 **15** Rather than react in panic to a challenging situation, allow yourself to pause and be calm so that the wiser options and alternatives within you have space to emerge.

16 Imagine you cast a carpet of flower petals out in front of you today and everywhere you walk is with equanimity and peace.

NOVEMBER

 17 Each day you awake to the gift of life. Appreciate this by engaging fully in your surroundings, with everyone you meet and in the tasks you undertake.

 18 Challenge yourself today to notice when you are impatient. Observe how you react to this and see if you can apply the wisdom of patience.

 19 Nurture your loved ones by telling them you love and appreciate them. Your words will boost their confidence and sense of well-being.

NOVEMBER

 20 Always be curious, because fostering wisdom is a lifelong process. Ask questions of others and of yourself.

 21 Slow down, concentrate on one thing at a time and be fully present in the moment. This will allow you to savour the enjoyable things and perform to your best abilities in your work.

 22 When you are reading an interesting book, don't keep it to yourself. Chat to people about what you have read and engage in discussion and sharing.

Believe nothing, no matter where you read it, or who said it, no matter if I have said it, unless it agrees with your own reason and your own common sense.

Buddha

24

Do not try to know everything, or you may end up knowing nothing.

Democritus

25 What pearl of wisdom would you share about your life with others? Search deeply for the buried treasure within.

 26 Make sure you are getting enough sleep. You will be able to perform your daily activities successfully and make decisions with greater clarity.

 27 If you dislike cleaning your house, put your favourite piece of music on and focus on the great exercise you will benefit from. A wise person knows how to get the job done whatever it takes!

NOVEMBER

 Cultivate a daily practice of being still and listening to your inner wisdom. Encourage yourself by finding a quiet place in your home where you can sit and be comfortable and calm.

 Make a delicious warming broccoli soup and enjoy the knowledge that it is improving your brainpower with its high levels of vitamin K.

 Simple wise words for today – if you are feeling overwhelmed with work or chores, make a list of your priorities. Follow the list and stay focused.

DECEMBER

 Remain open to possibilities even when things appear to be going wrong. Know that true wisdom is about picking yourself up when you have fallen down.

 Happiness is a decision you can make ahead of time. Seek the positive in everything today. Even if you are stuck in the post office queue get chatting and cheer everyone up!

DECEMBER

 Be a visionary and don't give up. Be clear about all the positive things you wish to include in your life and be willing to keep learning.

 Make plans for next year to go on a retreat or a sabbatical, giving you some time to learn more about yourself.

 Start today with the intention of keeping a clear conscience. Confucius, the sixth century Chinese philosopher, taught that this is a building block of wisdom.

Now there is one outstandingly important fact regarding Spaceship Earth, and that is that no instruction book came with it.

Buckminster Fuller

The key to the wisdom of inner meaning is in the knowledge and ability to distinguish the material world from the spiritual world.

Suhrawardi

Wisdom is not rooted in the desire for money and material goods but for peace and creativity. Be creative even if it's just a reshuffle of furniture in your house.

 Give a hug to a friend or family member as a way of showing support and love. The key to wisdom is being able to express yourself.

 Bring the spirit of flexibility with you into your day. If others resist your plans, be prepared to listen to what they are saying and be open to alternative ideas.

If you are out shopping today, consider whether you need new items or if you could repair what you still have. Our wise choices can save money and the planet.

 Allow yourself to appreciate and celebrate the magic of the festive season.

 If you feel a strong emotion, pause and be curious about it. Suppressing your feelings doesn't teach you anything but exploring and acknowledging them can provide a chance to understand yourself better.

Find humour in your circumstances, however challenging they might be. A sense of humour is a great strength, and laughter not only brings happiness but is proven to increase immunity and reduce stress.

 Notice how our lives tend to be habitually full of hastiness and speed. Today, why not try a slower pace interspersed with moments of tranquil stillness. What might you gain from this?

DECEMBER

 Book yourself a massage. It can increase your serotonin and dopamine levels that help to reduce depression and cheer you up. Listen to your inner wisdom to guide you in the care of your health.

 Travel outside your comfort zone as this provides a great learning opportunity, especially if you need to rely on your own resources to survive.

 Shine clarity onto your life by measuring how much you do for others and how much you do for yourself. If there is an unbalance, make plans to introduce you back into your life.

Not everything that counts
can be counted, and not
everything that can be
counted counts.

Albert Einstein

We can learn much from wise words, little from wisecracks, and less from wise guys.

William Arthur Ward

DECEMBER

 21 Sometimes you have to take a chance rather than playing it safe. Venture into the unknown to experience a little fear and a lot of learning. Think what you might do to challenge yourself.

 22 What we say, and do, to others can have more of an impact than we ever realise. Be aware of this today and look for opportunities to show kindness and consideration.

 23 All problems and challenges require the application of wisdom so when the time comes, ask yourself the question, 'Am I being wise?'

As you get involved in the seasonal festivities, remember that you are creating memories for all future tomorrows. Bring your full participation and joy to every moment.

Christmas Day: Set aside the need to control the perfect outcome and spend the day in laughter, love and enjoyment.

 Take notice of the wisdom that family members may share with you. An elderly relative may have an inspiring tale to tell and will enjoy your loving attention.

DECEMBER

 Share the wisdom you have learnt from growing up by becoming a mentor to a young person. Seek information about this on the Internet.

 If you are starting to think about making changes in your life, remember you'll progress further quicker if you start small so that you will achieve tiny successes upon which to build your confidence.

 There is plenty of wisdom around about healthy eating. Make a concerted effort to eat well and change some of your routines that have kept you in a rut.

30 It is said you cannot learn wisdom, you awaken to it. Allow this possibility by always believing in yourself.

New Year's Eve: Review the past twelve months to see if you have become a little wiser. Don't become disheartened if you haven't achieved the wisdom you would have liked. You are on the journey of a lifetime!

If you're interested in finding out more about our books, find us on Facebook at **Summersdale Publishers** and follow us on Twitter at **@Summersdale**.

www.summersdale.com